M000309204

What Now

Survival Guide for the
Blindsided and Brokenhearted

JUSTINA CHEN

Sparkline :: Story

What Now: Survival Guide for the Blindsided and Brokenhearted

Copyright © 2013 by Justina Chen

All rights reserved. No part of this book may be used or repro-duced in any manner whatsoever without written permission except in the case of brief quotations embodied in critical ar-ticles and reviews. Printed in the United States of America.

For information address: Sparkline :: Story, Attn: Rights and Per-missions Department, P.O. Box 103, Medina, WA 98039

10 9 8 7 6 5 4 3 2 1

Library of Congress Cataloguing-in-Publication Data

Chen, Justina

What Now: Survival Guide for the Blindsided and Brokenhearted / by Justina Chen

     p.   cm.

Summary: An incisive Survival Guide for women in the first 30 days after their relationship ends.

ISBN: 978-0-9887174-0-4

Design by Sugar Studios - sugarstudiosdesign.com

To all the women who have
walked this stony path
and all those who follow.

"Whether you turn to the right or to the left, your ears will hear a voice behind you, saying, 'This is the way, walk in it.'"

Isaiah 30:21

"History, despite its wrenching pain, cannot be unlived, but if faced with courage, need not be lived again."

Maya Angelou

Foreword: Blindsided

Y ou receive the call.

"Hey, we need to talk. So how does moving to China sound?" says the voice you've heard every day for the past fifteen years. The voice that vowed to love you for richer or poorer. This is a richer moment: an adventure you both have craved, a chance to live the extraordinary life you have both imagined, an experience that you have both wanted to bond you even closer to your children.

So you pull your kids out of school. You reduce your home to one hundred and thirty-four neatly packed boxes, filled with hopes and dreams for this new life. You watch the moving truck haul the boxes and furniture away where they will sail the ocean blue to your new home. There's a new language to learn. A new school to start. A new community to create. Not to mention, new customs to adopt and a new life to navigate.

Then eight weeks later, your furniture finally arrives after its long maiden voyage. You unpack the one hundred and thirty-four boxes, which at long last turns your cavernous new house into a semblance of home. Your kids settle in at their new school. You're enjoying your new life where twice weekly language lessons challenge you, visits to the grocery store are adventures, and every outing fills your creative pot.

Then, you receive The Call. It comes in the language you may have spoken your whole life, but somehow you no longer understand the words.

"We need to talk," says the voice that vowed to love you until death do you part. "I've been seeing someone for awhile."

And suddenly you find yourself alone in a foreign country and the unwitting co-star in a midlife cliché. Your stubborn heart may keep beating, but you feel dead inside. After the phone drops to the desk, you are hit with two terrible truths: your husband literally has loved you to death. And the adventure that was supposed to bond your family has broken you instead.

Four years later, I remember The Call with clarity. But those first thirty days afterward? Those are one big, messy, brokenhearted blur. I was so discombobulated, disoriented, and decision-impaired, it was all I could do to breathe, shower, and dress—let alone put food on the table, console the kids, and write my next novel.

"What now? What now? That was the question that pounded in my head and haunted my every mindless footstep in the days and daze ahead. All I wanted was someone to tell me what to do now because I had absolutely no clue."

What now? What now? That was the question that pounded in my head and haunted my every mindless footstep in the days and daze ahead. All I wanted was someone to tell me what to do now because I had absolutely no clue. Surely, the answer was in a book. But in China, I didn't have the luxury of a library or a bookstore stocked with books in English about being abandoned.

Even when I returned to the states, what I found were entire bookshelves crammed with sad titles about sad topics I never thought I'd experience firsthand: Recovering from an affair. Repairing broken trust. Divorcing after forty.

The titles alone exhausted me. How was I going to plow through three hundred pages of dense text when I could barely carry on a conversation?

What I wanted was a concise survival guide for what to do now in this barren land called betrayal that no woman I knew talked about. What do you do when you're left—and left with kids to support and a house to run by yourself? How am I supposed to put the kids and myself back together when I can't even get out of bed? What do I need to do now to safeguard myself and my children?

There is a concept called sistering that I write about in my novel, RETURN TO ME. When wood begins to rot, builders often flank it with a piece of healthy wood to keep a structure sound. That's what my friends and family did for me: they sistered me and my disintegrating life—especially in that first month.

They gathered around me and told me: come home, find your money, allow us to help you.

And that is what I would like to do for you: Take everything I learned from my team of family, friends, and experts—and sister you. Give you the *WHAT NOW Survival Guide* for those first traumatic thirty days after a crisis blindsides you and breaks your heart. These are your marching orders for what you can do now to take care of yourself and your kids—emotionally, physically, legally, and financially. These are your operating instructions to keep you standing long enough so you can take the next step, then the next. Because I remember how impossible it was to concen-

> *"These are your marching orders for what you can do now to take care of yourself and your kids—emotionally, physically, legally, and financially."*

trate, I've deliberately written this Survival Guide to be a short, quick read. The information is straightforward and the intent simple: to set you up to reclaim your life—leaving you better, not bitter.

To be frank: I am no expert in parenting or finances. Nor am I credentialed as a counselor or physician. But I am a woman who has trekked this path before you, guided by smart and caring women and men before me. I am a woman who got up on my feet—not always gracefully, but always faithfully—when betrayal cut me down. I am a woman who survived that first month... and the many long months after that.

So, too, will you.

In the back of this book, you will find a list of resources, books and websites by trusted experts who delve much more deeply and knowledgably into each subject covered in this Survival Guide. Read those later or alongside this one as you are able.

For now, regardless of what happens in your future— perhaps this ordeal will strengthen your marriage, perhaps not—your number one job is to keep yourself and your children safe right now. Your number one goal is to set the foundation so that you get through this crisis with your heart, soul, children, health, and finances intact. Your number one responsibility is to survive this initial upheaval in your life.

Here's what you can do when you despair to yourself, WHAT NOW?

Justina Chen
January, 2013

Table of Contents

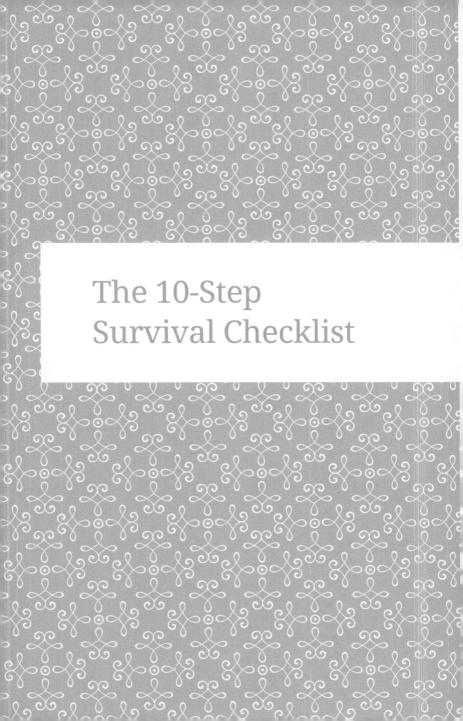

The 10-Step
Survival Checklist

1 Commit to face this ordeal with
   strength and grace.

2 See your Ob-Gyn. Now.

3 Select one or two trusted secret keepers who
   can safeguard your confidences, tell you the
   truth, and help you process your emotions.

4 Assure your kids that they—and you—will be fine.

5 Account for all your money and
   cut your spending.

6 Find a safe haven.

7 Assemble your team: lawyer, accountant, financial adviser, and counselor.

8 Ask for help.

9 Nourish yourself as you would a dear friend.

10 Practice gratitude.

CHAPTER ONE

Set Your Intention

"Be bold and strong, banish fear
and doubt, for the Lord, your God is
with you wherever you go."

Joshua 1:9

*H*ours after finding out that my husband was leaving us to start a new life with his secretary in China, I remember my kids asking, "When's Dad coming home?" I remember not knowing what to say. I remember putting the kids to bed. I remember catching a glimpse of myself in the mirror, looking and feeling older than Methuselah—my body worn out and my soul worn down. And I remember sinking into the bathtub as if I were literally drowning in my sorrow.

No amount of hot bath water could stop my shaking. So I hauled myself out—careful to avoid the mirror—and powered on my computer to seek my closest friends who were eight long time zones away. Waiting for me in my inbox was a message from an early reader of my novel, NORTH OF BEAUTIFUL. And what she wrote was this: For the first time in her life, she could stand in front of a mirror and feel beautiful.

I knew at that moment that God had me cupped tenderly in His palm and that I would be fine—especially when three words sang in my mind: Better, not bitter. This would become my guiding principle for the next long year. I vowed to shape this ordeal into an opportunity to become a better person, not a bitter one.

What is your intention going to be?

STRATEGIES TO DETERMINE YOUR INTENTION:

- Wherever you find your spiritual comfort and sustenance—whether it is God or the Universe,

in nature or a yoga class, in prayer or meditation—seek it now. You will need to gather all
your strength to survive these first thirty days.

- Even as your world is upending, set your intention for how you will get through your ordeal.
  Your intention establishes the very foundation for how you will act, respond, navigate,
  and negotiate through one of the most difficult
  periods in your life. While you did not choose
  to have your life shattered, you can choose how
  you will rebuild yourself. While you did not
  choose this betrayal, you can choose the kind
  of person you become: the wronged one or the
  stronger one.

  Perhaps you will vow to practice grace through
  this crisis. Or to behave with the strength of your
  values so you will feel proud two years from now,

twenty years from now, and on your deathbed.

Or perhaps you'll vow to love yourself through this ordeal and to treat yourself as kindly as you would a good friend. Or to learn everything that you can from this experience. Or to hold true to yourself and your ethics. Or perhaps it's simply to learn to ask for help.

If you have children, perhaps your intention is to be their rock and to make sure they feel utterly beloved...no matter what.

• Whatever your intention, set it now. Commit it to paper. Display the words in a place where they will sing you awake and lull you to sleep. This intention will be your North Star.

- A note about e-rants. Your harsh insults can come back and haunt you. Use your integrity and strength so that you—as best you're able—can deal with every issue in a manner that would hold up according to your values—and in court. As one friend said, "Rants to a baseball team that your husband is a jerk don't actually help." So turn to your close friends for those necessary blowups and fits, but keep your emotional meltdowns off the computer.

Just remember: you are the hero of your story. Terrible things happen to all heroes—but that is why they're heroes. Regardless of the trial and setback and failure, every hero is responsible for choosing how he or she responds. And every hero prevails.

CHAPTER TWO

Health

"Health is a state of complete physical,
mental and social well-being,
and not merely the absence of disease
or infirmity."

World Health Organization

A friend told me that over the course of several affairs, her dad had infected her mom with a few STDs. Frankly, the thought of getting tested for STDs hadn't even crossed my mind. But who knew that "with my body, I thee worship" would also mean "oh, and I also worshipped somebody else's body, too."

Who also knew it was possible to drop fifteen pounds in three weeks? Or that it would take my body three years to recover from its sustained fight-or-flight mode, which included losing clumps of hair, battling insomnia, enduring the indignity of acne, and feeling perpetually weary.

How are you taking care of yourself?

STRATEGIES TO SAFEGUARD YOUR HEALTH:

- Make an appointment with your Ob-Gyn now. If you don't have a gynecologist, head to a clinic pronto. Do not even consider procrastinating.

- When booking the appointment, it's essential to underscore your urgency. A simple explanation will suffice: "I just found out that my partner cheated on me, and I am really scared. I need to be tested for STDs. How soon can you fit me in?"

- Snag the first available appointment.

- At the appointment, ask if the test results can be expedited at no additional cost.

- Beg the doctor or nurse to phone you right away with the results, please!

- Refrain from having revenge sex. There's nothing more self-destructive now than to put yourself deliberately in harm's way. As my doctor intoned, the largest at-risk group for AIDS is women over forty.

- Once you've taken all the STD tests, there is nothing to be gained by fretting and worrying. Try your very hardest to set aside any angst about what the results will be. Have peace that you have done everything you can to safeguard your health for now.

- Seek a counselor, priest, pastor, therapist, or wise friend to help you process this emotional avalanche from a psychological and spiritual perspective. From leaning on your faith community to your children's school counselor, you need to gain strength from true wisdom for yourself and your kids.

- Make sure you take care of your mental health. I'm not talking retail therapy or spa treatments. As good as they make you feel, those benefits are temporary. So take care of yourself in a deep, soulful way. Find time for daily prayer or meditation, journaling or listening to music. Or simply sitting and staying still. Whatever gives you pause and peace, consider it sacred time for yourself.

- Eat well. Your body is most likely in a fight-or-flight mode, which means it believes that it's endangered. Nourish your body with nutritious food as you would if you were training for a marathon. In the span of three weeks, I dropped fifteen pounds. My shower floor was carpeted with hair. So force yourself to eat well, even if you have lost your appetite, and especially if ice cream is the only food group that sounds vaguely appealing. Consider keeping a cup of cheerios or trail mix in the car to encourage nibbling.

- Sleep. As impossible as it may feel to sleep, it's important to get your rest. You need your wits

about you for this next leg of your life. Consider consulting your doctor for advice about
how best to weather your ordeal. Mine ran me
through the effects of stress I should expect my
body to experience, told me what was in the
range of normal, and made sure I knew what
symptoms would demand his attention. Talk to
your health care provider regarding temporary
medication or other remedies if your sleepless-
ness persists.

- Keep your body fit and strong with daily ex-
ercise. The last thing your kids and you can
afford right now is for you to fall ill.

CHAPTER THREE

Who to Tell, What to Say

"A cruel story runs on wheels,
and every hand oils the wheels as they run."

Ouida

A few days after finding myself and the kids alone in China, one of our neighbors came over. Without much fanfare, Pam sat next to me and said, "I heard the news, and I actually don't want to know the details."

She paused, letting her words sink in to the sea sponge that had once been my brain.

What? I thought, stunned. She didn't want to hear the details when I so needed to talk to someone about what had happened? To rage at the unfairness? To share my fears?

Instead Pam said, "I've been through my own tragedy. And I have some advice for you. Be very careful of who you talk to and how much you tell people."

Wise words, which I disregarded once. In a weak, lonely moment, I poured my story out to an acquaintance who had descended on my home like a vulture scenting the fresh carcass of gossip. After I shared the intimate details and received her sunny-weather comfort, I never heard from her again.

It is natural and tempting to divulge every last salacious detail to any sympathetic ear. Resist the urge. People are already going to gossip; why provide the oh-so-pungent fertilizer?

And once you find your circle of secret keepers, then release yourself to them.

STRATEGIES TO CREATE YOUR SUPPORT NETWORK:

- Entrust the details to a very small inner circle of best friends. Nobody else needs to know—or has earned the privilege to hear—the gory details of your betrayal. If you would be mortified to overhear complete strangers dissecting the details of your personal crisis in a coffee shop, then confide only in your one or two trusted secret keepers.

- Even though most people who ask you what's going on are just concerned and want to help, no one outside your inner circle needs to know everything.

- If you don't want your kids to hear all the juicy details—or to have them talked about at school— that's all the more reason to protect your privacy.

- Gossip has a way of boomeranging back to hurt you and the kids in unexpected ways that you cannot control or foresee. So don't fuel its momentum.

- Refrain from any public lambasting or making a scene. The only person it reflects badly upon will be you.

Cry out! Don't be stolid and silent with your pain. Lament! And let the milk of loving flow into you.

Rumi

- Create a one-line explanation of your situation that shuts down any further prying and ends a conversation you don't want to have—but is still polite and gracious. Try this: "Thanks so much for caring. As you can imagine, things are pretty rough now. So I appreciate your support."

CHAPTER FOUR

Your Kids

"If you have only one smile in you,
give it to the people you love."

Maya Angelou

*Three months into what was supposed to be a one-year,
and potentially two-year, stint in China, the kids and I
found ourselves jerked back abruptly to the states. I will
never forget my children's faces when they found their
best friends waiting for them at the airport: This was
tangible proof that they were safe at home.*

*Your most important job as a mother during these
first thirty days is to ensure as much stability as*

possible for the kids. And to assure them that every-

thing will turn out just fine...even if you have your

own doubts.

What do your kids need now?

"*Love begins by taking care of the closest
ones—the ones at home.*"
-Mother Teresa

STRATEGIES TO STABILIZE YOUR KIDS:

- Your children need an age-appropriate neutral
  divorce story, an explanation about what's hap-
  pening to their family that they can understand.
  Please note that this isn't about constructing
  a fantasy or creating a fictional account of the
  breakdown between you and their father. And

this certainly isn't about sharing sordid details to demonize the other parent. This is about crafting an explanation of the new family circumstances in a way that protects their emotional safety, security, and childhood from the drama of difficult adult realities. There will be plenty of time later for a more encompassing story when your kids are old enough, mature enough, and have enough life experience to make sense of complex adult issues.

- If you don't have a routine, now's the time to establish one. If you have a routine, keep it. Both the kids and you will benefit from a schedule as you slog through these first few weeks. So be clear and deliberate about the time to wake up, fall into bed, do homework, tackle housework, shop for groceries, and more.

- If possible, keep the connections that stabilize your children, especially relationships with their relatives on both sides and their relationship with the other parent. Perhaps pets provide your children with comfort. Consider allowing them to take their pets wherever they go.

- Organization is going to be your key to survival this month. If you're having problems keeping track of details (say, you forget to pick up your kids from school...), ask a highly organized friend to help you think through all the logistics. This is especially important if you find that you are single parenting. When do the kids need to be at school? How will they get there? How are they getting home? How are they getting to their activities?

- When it comes to breaking down in front of the kids, practice the 80/20 rule. The fact is: you will fall apart in front of them when you least expect it. But the kids need you to be their rock, the solid adult who's confident that all will be well. So as a rule of thumb, 80% of your breakdowns should be done with your best friends or in private. That said, it's perfectly okay for children to know that you're "sad, too," "this is *really* tough," and "we'll all get through it."

- Promise yourself that you will act civilly with their father whether in public or in private simply because it is in your kids' best interest to keep warring to a minimum.

- Inform the teachers and principal about your situation so they can watch over your kids at school—and alert you if there's any backlash behavior. (But again, remember: no one at school needs to know the intimate details of the betrayal. A concise one or two sentences is sufficient.)

- Check if the school provides counseling or support groups, and consider signing up your kids for this service.

- Consider having a friend take photos of you and the kids. I know—it sounds crazy especially when you probably have bags under your eyes from insomnia, but those photographs are a powerful visual statement that you are still a family. (A friend suggested this to me; her mom did the same some thirty years ago when her dad left. I'm so glad she shared this healing

idea with me. Some of my most cherished photographs are the ones taken of myself and the
kids on our last day in China. We look so united
and strong.)

- "Rebrand" yourself and the kids. This was an
  idea I grabbed from my days as a marketing
  manager. A few weeks after everything happened, the kids and I created a "nickname" for
  the three of us based on our names. To this
  day, we refer to ourselves with this new handle.
  Renaming is a powerful and symbolic way to
  signal to the kids that while you may be a different family, you are a complete family.

CHAPTER FIVE

Follow the Money

"An investment in knowledge
pays the best dividends."

Benjamin Franklin

"Where's all your money?" a girlfriend asked me on the day of The Call. She was positioned at her computer, fingers over the keyboard, ready to be my forensic accountant. "This can't be it."

My friend and I both stared at the total amount in the joint Schwab account, an amount that couldn't have been all that was saved after fifteen years of hard work. I was embarrassed to answer: "I don't know."

Seriously, how was it possible that I could graduate with honors in Economics from Stanford and have shockingly little knowledge about my financial situation?

"Find out," she said firmly, already toggling to a new tab for the airlines. "You need to fly home as soon as you can to find your money."

Easier said than done. Where would I begin when I didn't even know any of our other bank account numbers, passwords, nothing? Besides, I was so disoriented that first day, my girlfriend had to book my tickets from Shanghai back to Seattle. So what chance did I have to assess my financial picture?

Luckily, another girlfriend was then a personal wealth investor at Goldman Sachs. She answered my SOS call from China, cleared her calendar for my return, and promised to step me through exactly how to figure out my financial situation.

What is your financial position right now?

STRATEGIES TO ASSESS YOUR FINANCES:

- Agree with your partner to freeze your accounts so there's no land grab for money—and no huge expenditures by either party now.

- Allocate an equal amount of money for both of you to live on for at least the next thirty days.

- If you don't have any idea of how to find out where your money is, consider asking a trusted friend or family member who's on top of his / her finances to assist you.

- Best set aside one full day to do this forensic CSI work.

- Pull all your online and paper files from your checking, savings, and investment accounts. As well, you will want to pull together your files for your credit cards, debit cards, mortgage and other loans. (You may need paper copies of these later if you go to divorce. So you might as well print everything out now.)

- Remember that at this moment, you aren't looking for A+ perfection nor are you chasing down every last penny. You just need a generally accurate assessment of how much you and your partner have as assets and debts.

CHAPTER SIX

Safe Haven

"The ache of home lives in all of
us, the safe place where we can
go as we are and not be questioned."

Maya Angelou

Friends were housesitting for us while we lived in China. Bless their generous hearts; they didn't just vacate when they heard the kids and I were returning home, but they stocked the refrigerator and scrubbed every last crevice of my home. Then, a few days after our return, another group of friends repainted the front entry so that I could reclaim my space and purge the house of any painful mementos. They unpacked our luggage, prepared dinner, and rejuvenated the flowerpots as if promising me a future blooming.

STRATEGIES TO RECLAIM YOUR SPACE:

- If you're leaving an abusive relationship, do whatever it takes to keep yourself safe. (See Resources.)

- Consider changing the locks if you will feel violated should your partner barge into your home unannounced.

- Consider leaving your home for a few days if it's too painful to be there with all your memories and mementos. Retreat to a family member or friend's home. The kids and I stayed with my parents for a week.

- Ask a friend or two to remove all your wedding photos and other painful mementos from your home: pictures, keepsakes, gifts, etc. Store all these items in a box for the future when you're ready to deal with them. While you might want to throw those sentimental items away—or burn them, just remember that your kids and grandkids might want them one day. So archive them away.

- Cut yourself slack if you don't have energy to clean your home to shining perfection. Of course, if you calm yourself by doing house-work, by all means, clean or iron or whatever you do to get to your zen spot.

- If you're handling the household repairs by yourself now, make an appointment with a house inspector—the same one you'd hire to inspect a new home you want to buy. Ask him or her to conduct a top-to-bottom inspection of your home, and tell you exactly what needs repairing and when.

CHAPTER SEVEN

Budget

"A big part of financial freedom
is having your heart and mind
free from worry about the what-ifs of life."

Suze Orman

Two of my financial guru friends urged me to pare my budget to the bare minimum until my life settled down. Their thinking: I should maintain as much capital as possible to take me through this crisis for as long as possible. Wise advice. As it turned out after a review of my financial picture, I had to return to work. But by living frugally in the early months, I had the cushion to spend the time I needed to stabilize my kids and find an unexpectedly good job.

STRATEGIES FOR A BUDGET DIET:

- Apply now for your own credit card if you don't already have one. You want to establish your own credit history.

- Live frugally to maintain as much of your capital as you can while you sort out your financial situation. You may be able to keep your house, but then again, the hard truth is that your mortgage and your lifestyle simply may not be achievable post-divorce. Your goal should be to minimize all of your monthly payments now so that if alimony or child support payments cease, you will not be forced to move.

- Be extremely honest and diligent about tracking how much you spend a month—and determine what you can cut immediately. For the

near-term, curtail any discretionary spending.
For instance, you may want to put your coffee
shop habit on hold, stop seeing movies in the-
aters, and limit dining at restaurants.

- Forego revenge spending. My sister took me
  out shopping right after it became clear just
  how much my spouse had splurged on his girlfriend. But you know what? I don't wear a single thing that I bought in that shopping spree,
  not then, not now. There's no joy in wearing
  any of those beautiful items because they're
  tainted with memories of an excruciating time
  in my life. Much better to save your money.
  (That said, it could be very therapeutic to buy
  yourself all new underwear. Just saying...)

- Renegotiate every recurring charge you have from utilities to waste collection to cable service to cell phone service. Force yourself to assess and act upon a different bill every other day until you have scrutinized them all. Simply explain your situation to the customer service rep, ask for help, and be open to cutting features. For instance, an opening line can be: "I'm single parenting now and have to watch my every penny. Can you please help me figure out ways to cut my bill?" Thirty dollars saved here, twenty dollars saved there, all adds up.

CHAPTER EIGHT

Your Team

"For beautiful eyes, look for the good
in others; for beautiful lips, speak only
words of kindness; and for poise, walk with
the knowledge that you are never alone."

Audrey Hepburn

As much as I wanted to believe that my marriage could be repaired, I also knew that I had to take some precautions to protect my children and myself. My spouse "wanted out"—and had conducted the affair for some time, an affair he had bankrolled with our joint account. I had no idea how long he'd been planning for a divorce or how much of a headstart he had on the process. So I had to begin to assemble my team—divorce lawyer, financial advisor, and accountant—just in case things didn't work out as I had hoped. At the very least, I knew I needed a counselor for myself and my kids—someone with insight and wisdom to shepherd us through the ordeal.

In this first month, you don't need to run out and snag a lawyer. But what you can do is prepare yourself.

Who do you want to recruit for your team?

STRATEGIES TO ASSEMBLE YOUR BEST TEAM:

- Check your health insurance to see if counseling is covered for yourself and your kids—and by all means, explain your situation as you ask for help.

- See if your children's school provides counseling and use that resource, too. Family service agencies will often offer services on a sliding fee scale.

- Scout for your best team. You can start by making a list of all your friends and acquaintances who have landed well post-divorce: they're happy, healthy, strong, and emanate a forgiving spirit. Then ask those people for their honest assessments of their team, including a counselor.

- Be steely-eyed about your legal road ahead. Will lawyers be in play? Is your spouse / partner prepared to fight or does he want a quick exit? Perhaps he hopes to work together with you in the best interest of the children. Whatever your situation, it's imperative that you pick a legal team and strategy that best represents you and your goals. Look for a strategist who has a clear view of your specific situation and can assess the legal challenges ahead.

- Get referrals from trusted friends and other professionals. Book interviews with at least two or three divorce lawyers, especially if you know your spouse has already done so. A one-hour consult should be free or provided at a nominal charge. You want to ensure you secure an astute lawyer who hears what you are saying and is working in tandem with your goals. The last thing you need is a lawyer who will antagonize your spouse or escalate the situation.

- This is a good time to revisit your intention statement (see Chapter One) and to act from a place of integrity. Remember that your soon-to-be-ex-spouse will forever be your business partner in co-parenting your children.

- Ask one friend or family member to interview the divorce lawyers with you—and to take notes during the meeting for you. Your mental state might be as foggy as someone who has just learned that she has cancer, meaning your judgment and decision-making might be impaired. You may not be able to process any information clearly. Plus, if you've been blindsided by the affair, you may not trust your own intuition and people judging skills.

- And finally, you need to think less like a wife and more like a business executive, objectively assessing your present, future, and retirement needs. Your team will be working for your long-term security. So be sure you take into account health care, college costs, and any additional education you personally may need in order to become independent.

- Tap your friends for help, from the financial whiz who can review your budget to the caravans of SUVs to move you if you must relocate. Don't be afraid or feel too proud to reach out for help. Trust me, you will be amazed at how much assistance your friends want to provide.

CHAPTER NINE

Outsource Your Memory

"When you are tense and your mind
is overstimulated or distracted, your
ability to remember can suffer. Stress
caused by an emotional trauma
can also lead to memory loss."

WebMD

For at least a year, my memory was missing in action.
Countless times, I'd find myself driving aimlessly, forget-
ting where I was going. Or even worse, I would get lost
driving home from the neighborhood grocery store that I
had frequented for the past fifteen years.

One of my strengths has always been my organiza-
tional skills. That, too, became another victim during
my ordeal. I floundered at project management, couldn't
multitask, and failed to remember crucial details. It was

as if the entire prefrontal area of my brain—the part responsible for working memory, attention, and problem solving—went on strike.

STRATEGIES TO OUTSOURCE YOUR MEMORY:

- Write everything down either on your Smartphone or in a notebook. Consider setting alarms for important to-dos. Otherwise, you may forget meetings, appointments, tasks, bills, deadlines, and commitments.

- Apologize in advance to your friends and family for forgetting important dates and failing to follow through on commitments. Ask them to remind you gently during this first month of your plans with them.

- Designate a box to house all the documents for your ordeal. Print out any email or document that pertains to your finances or spouse, and throw the paper into The Box. You can always file the papers later if you're not up to it now. The important thing is to keep your records in one spot in case you need that information later. You'll be surprised at the vast black hole that is your memory and how quickly you forget where you placed important documents.

- Ask a trusted friend or family member to attend any important meetings with you so they can take notes and ask questions you might not remember to ask. As well, they can help you process the topics covered in the meeting, be your sounding board, and strategize your next steps.

CHAPTER TEN

Your Mental Health

"The art of knowing
is knowing what to ignore."

Rumi

Over the course of the ordeal, my mind and heart would reel from everything thrown at me from "If you hadn't insisted on moving to China, the affair wouldn't have happened" to "I never felt loved by you" and "Yeah, you showed me in actions you loved me, but you never said it in words." But those words were nothing compared to the self-flagellation I administered so well to myself: all the things I should have said and done to be a better wife. All the ways I could have supported him better. All the ways

I could have showered him with love.

And then, of course, I went through the machinations of providing a logical excuse to explain the affair. He had a mental breakdown. An undiagnosed case of bipolar disorder. A brain tumor. How else could a good, kind man tear apart our family? Move us all to China? Then leave us eight weeks after we uprooted ourselves?

Facing the truth about our own weaknesses, transgressions, and failures is the good, hard work needed for self-

"The truth will set you free."
-John 8:32

growth. But as you're doing your internal soul-searching, you need a balanced viewpoint of Reality. None of what has happened to you is entirely the fault of any one person—not you, not even the one who left. 100% blame on either party is simply not the calculus of life or lost

*love or even betrayal. And it's certainly not the fertile
ground that you'll want and need for forgiveness in the
years to come.*

STRATEGIES FOR CONFRONTING THE TRUTH:

- Remind yourself daily of the intention you set
  for facing this ordeal.

- Create a list of the Truths about the situation if
  your mind starts racing with should haves and
  could haves—or if you hear too much self-in-
  flicted blame or fault-finding from other people. Write down the facts. For instance, "Truth:
  I dedicated an entire book to him, words written in love" or "Truth: I told him I would support him and his career" or "Truth: I wanted to
  move to Siena, not Shanghai."

- Create a list of Truths about yourself, both your strengths and weaknesses. For instance, "Truth: I love faithfully" or "Truth: I have a temper when I feel disrespected."

- Review those Truth Statements with your counselor if you are having doubts about your reality.

- Reread those Truth Statements whenever you start attacking yourself. And reread them when you feel like attacking your spouse / partner.

- Step away from the computer whenever you feel like you're about to rage at your spouse / partner...or even grovel. Return to your intention and to your truths first before responding to any email.

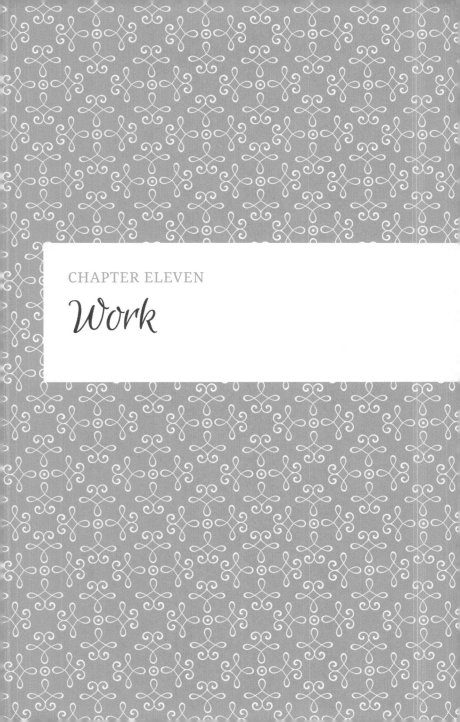

CHAPTER ELEVEN

Work

"Every tomorrow has two handles.
We can take hold of it with the
handle of anxiety or the handle of faith."

Henry Ward Beecher

This is my mind on the drug called anxiety when I learned that I had to rejoin the workforce: "Oh, my gosh! The last time I worked, cell phones weighed three pounds and my wicked cool laptop clocked in at seventeen pounds! I'm a novelist! I've been a writer-mom for fourteen years! No one is looking for a novelist! I've never seen a 'Help wanted: novelist' sign. I have no marketable skills other than organizing bake sales and talking to made-up characters! And I am old! What am I going to do?"

And so on. And on.

Perhaps you're already working full-time or part-time outside of the house—and are now juggling being a single parent on top of all your responsibilities. Perhaps after reviewing your finances, it's become painfully obvious that you will have to rejoin the workforce and you've been a stay-at-home mom.

Remind yourself: step by step. You're not being asked to land a job this minute or to be a superstar employee. All you're being asked this month is to ground yourself.

STRATEGIES TO PRESERVE YOUR SANITY IF YOU HAVE A JOB OUTSIDE THE HOME:

- Prevail upon friends to provide meals for at least the first week until you can get yourself into a routine. (I will never forget the generosity and thoughtfulness of a good friend who dropped off three frozen meals on the first week I started working.)

- Let your manager know what's going on in your personal life. Use your one-sentence synopsis. Be clear about what you need in this first month while you get yourself oriented: perhaps you need to leave work at five o'clock on the dot. Perhaps you need a project reassigned from you. Or a deadline extension. Ask for what you need.

- Don't allow yourself to worry about the long-term impact upon your career. Remind yourself that your job is to get through this month. That is all.

SELF-PRESERVATION STRATEGIES FOR THOSE
WHO NEED TO FIND EMPLOYMENT:

- Remind yourself that your first priority in this
  first month is to get your kids and yourself
  settled. That is all that is being asked of you
  this month. So if you have the means to do so,
  set your need to find a job aside until Month
  Two.

- If you have young children, it may make sense
  to hold off returning to work for a grace period
  to allow them to adjust. Also, additional time
  will enable you to better gauge how they're
  coping with their new family situation.

- Give yourself a timeframe if you need to go
  back to work. But if you can, be mindful of how

much time you'll need to take care of things legally and to help your child/children with all the immediate changes in your lives.

- Start the mechanics of networking. Reach out to your five most career-savvy friends and let them know your situation. Again, you don't need to go into details. Just let them know you'd appreciate an hour of their time to get their career advice. You can always book these meetings for Month Two if you're not up to this task right now.

- Collect information to update your resume. Start jotting down notes about all of your work and volunteer experience. Reach out to friends who have recently landed themselves a new job. Ask if they might be able to share their resumes with you as a template to build your own.

CHAPTER TWELVE

Gratitude

"Gratitude bestows reverence, allowing
us to encounter everyday epiphanies, those
transcendent moments of awe that change
forever how we experience life and the world."

John Milton

*Let's face it: losing heart and getting discouraged is
almost synonymous with ordeals. That said, research
shows that practicing gratitude can increase a person's
happiness by 25%. And I believe that gratitude inocu-
lates you from becoming bitter. Though the notion of
being happy ever again might seem totally impossible to
fathom, counting your blessings is a prelude to joy.*

Topping my gratitude list were my kids, brave and beau-

tiful through the entire ordeal—my son who fixed an overflowing toilet because he didn't want me to deal with the mess. My daughter who encouraged me, "Mom, aren't you glad that you aren't with a guy who cheated on you for the rest of your life?" My father who pored through financial statements. My mom who cooked for me. My friends who filled my home with new art made with their own hands, hired a parenting coach for me, took me on walks, checked in with daily texts, sent encouraging notes, deployed their teen boys to help me move my furniture, and cried with me on the phone.

With so many beautiful blessings in the midst of my trial, how could I not see that happiness was completely possible and that life still held so much joy?

STRATEGIES FOR REMEMBERING YOUR BLESSINGS:

- Keep a journal not just to process your anger and grief and fears, but to list all your gratitudes for the day. Aim to describe at least three blessings a day. Once you get in the habit of being actively grateful, you will be surprised at the outpouring of all the big and little ways that prove you are being cared for daily.

- Make a promise to yourself that you will mark the day of your anniversary—or any other sentimental day that you want to reclaim—with an email to every single person whose actions and words made you grateful during your ordeal. That is a powerful gift not just to the community who surrounded you with love, but for yourself.

What Next

> I said to my soul, be still, and let the
> dark come upon you. Which shall be
> the darkness of God. . . .
> So the darkness shall be the light,
> and the stillness the dancing.
> — T. S. Eliot

In the first thirty days after I learned about the affair, my heart felt as if it had been ground down to dust, and a single puff of wind would scatter my shattered self far, far from me. In the span of a single phone call, my well-planned life had turned into a crazy spinning top, whirling around aimlessly.

But then.

Almost a year to the day we moved to China, I read about the Pleiades meteor showers, which would be clearly seen that evening in Seattle. So at midnight, two girlfriends and I headed out to seek a remote clearing an hour away from town. We ended up on a golf course. Not the atmospheric meadow we had imagined, but we figured, it would still afford us a perfect, unobstructed view of the meteors as they streaked across the night sky. While we lay on the hood of the car, eyes pointed heavenward, chatting about wild adventures in high school, I realized something miraculous: I was happy.

Somewhere along my journey, the dust of my married life had been transformed into the stardust of a new life. And I was no longer spinning in a crazy daze anymore. I was dancing.

May the dust of your life become stardust, glorious and unimaginably beautiful. And may you once more dance with true joy.

And when that day of dancing comes—because it will—may you sister another traveller who finds herself on this unexpected journey.

Resources

CHAPTER ONE: SET YOUR INTENTION

When Your Heart Waits by Sue Monk Kidd
The Gifts of Imperfection by Brene Brown

CHAPTER TWO: HEALTH

http://www.cdc.gov/std/

http://www.mayoclinic.com/health/std-testing/ID00047

CHAPTER FOUR: YOUR KIDS

Mom's House, Dad's House For Kids by Isolina Ricci
Putting Children First: Proven Parenting Strategies for Helping Children Through Divorce by JoAnne Pedro-Carroll

CHAPTER FIVE: FOLLOW THE MONEY

Women and Money: Owning the Power to Control Your Destiny by Suze Orman

CHAPTER SIX: HOME IS YOUR SAFE HAVEN

National Domestic Violence Hotline, thehotline.org, 800-799-SAFE

CHAPTER SEVEN: BUDGET

Millionaire Teacher: The Nine Rules of Wealth You Should Have Learned in School by Andrew Hallam

CHAPTER EIGHT: YOUR TEAM

The International Academy of Collaborative Practitioners maintains a website that makes it easy to find collaborative practitioners by state, city, and in different disciplines (attorney, coach, etc.): www.collaborativepractice.com

CHAPTER TEN: THE TRUTH

After the Affair by Janis Abrahms Spring

CHAPTER ELEVEN: WORK

Steering by Starlight by Martha Beck

CHAPTER TWELVE: GRATITUDE

The Joy Diet by Martha Beck

The Single Mom's Devotional: A Book of 52 Practical and Encouraging Devotionals by Carol Floch

CPSIA information can be obtained at www.ICGtesting.com
Printed in the USA
BVOW101425060513

319863BV00002B/2/P